DEDICATION

Firstly, to Jesus my Lord and Saviour without whom I would not be able to have written this book, He is my rock and fortress in times of trouble. It says in the Bible in Jeremiah chapter 29 "For I know the plans I have for you, declares The Lord, plans to prosper you and not to harm you, plans to give you hope and a future."

To my family, who instilled in me from a young age that I can accomplish any task I set my heart and mind to.

To my dearest of friends Nick, Danni & Baby Wyatt, Whom I love and cherish beyond measure,

To Tracey Jones an amazing friend and the most wonderful of humans you could ever wish to meet.

To Jennifer Jones a great example of grace and kindness

And to Bella, Ruby & Pedro whose unconditional love made me the dog lover I never knew I was.

Introduction

Life holds in its hands many wonders, in the most subtle of places,

we have all heard the phrase " taking life for granted" and we often do.

many of my poems come from a place of ordinary, yet within the ordinary sometimes, just sometimes we become aware of something or someone special.

A small glimpse of wonder and beauty, A young child walking for the first time, A single parent overcoming obstacles and accomplishing something, anything, against all the odds, the drug addict or alcoholic beating their addiction, A cancer patient beating the disease.

Waves crashing on the shoreline or lightening painting the skies with its purple blueish hue.

Life is beautiful my friends if only we would take a moment, to pause, to take a step back and breathe and simply take time to notice it.

So be kind to each other and hold each other up in love.

Peace and blessings

Bryan Gwyn Headon

Contents

Touching You

When I'm feeling lonely or down

Or when I need a friend,

but there is no-one around

When I feel life being torn at the seams

And when I think hope is lost

and I'm losing my dreams

What I need is to be touching you.

The Rose

Standing in the garden
between two apple trees
There stands a rose, so delicate
As it sways within the breeze.

Blood red petals open wide
Revealing such a heart
To see it standing so alone
Alone throughout the dark.

Darkness comes and covers
The rose upon the ground
Until the light of dawn appears
And things once lost are found.

Lost

Lost in a world that is alien

Silently she cries

From mental pain and torment

She wipes her tired eyes.

Things that she did years ago

She remembers them quite well

But what she's done with her cup of tea

I'm afraid she couldn't tell.

Who cares

The old man sits on the old porch

In his old rocking chair

Smoking his pipe and sitting in peace

As he asks himself, who cares?

Who cares that I'm old and can't do what I used to

Who gives a thought of the times I feel low

who gives me help with the things I don't know

Oh, when will they care for me.

"What else can I say except think for a while

about the old folk just like me"

God Cares

When we go off on our own mindless ways

When we lose sight of our goals and oft go astray

When we feel nothing, we are doing is right

God cares.

When we are feeling like no-one is there

No-one to listen and no-one to share

When all around us feels so strange

God cares.

He knows all our weakness and sorrow

He feels all our hurt and our pain

He sent his son to die for man

To die for sinners slain

And through it all God cares.

Adam's Apple

After God created Adam

He made him a wife named Eve

In the cool of the evening, they went for a stroll

When the serpent began to deceive.

Apples for sale he hissed at her

Eve just couldn't refuse

Granny smiths or American reds

He asked with a smile on his face.

"But of the tree of the knowledge of good and evil,

thou shalt not eat of it: for in the day that thou eatest thereof

thou shalt surely die."

Genesis 2 verse 17

Wales

When God created England

He thought it quite a scream

To turn a pack of fifteen blokes

Into a rugby team.

But they knew not much of anything

They knew not much at all

They couldn't have a Propper game

They couldn't find the ball.

But then God had a brilliant idea

A tale that would beat all other tales

He would make a better team of course

And simply call them Wales.

The Valley

The valley is quiet now

The miners have all gone

No sound of colliers laughing

The landscape lies forlorn.

It's all gas and electric now

No-one bothers much with coal

Will Morris is a butcher

And Dai is on the dole.

The families are all leaving

The valley lies bereft

The towns lay eerie, silent

For no industry is left.

Casual Christianity

Amid the lawlessness and violence

Through the torture and the pain

Through the Insanity of mindlessness

They are calling out your name.

Asking for your blessings

yet their hearts are fixed on greed

While people all around them

Are so desperately in need.

Brother killing brother

For a nickel or a dime

Stepping over the folk on the floor

To get to their meeting on time.

The Dock

I stand in the dock convicted
Of a grave and a serious crime
The crime was becoming a Christian
And soon I'll be doing the time.

They asked me to swear on the bible
But I read them a scripture instead
The judge asked me "why did you do it"
"There wasn't a gun to your head"

He asked for a reason or motive
I said, "It was love, can't you see?"
The love of a man like no other
Who hung upon calvary's tree.

The judge shouted "order", The court became still
His face became redder, He looked rather ill
He stood with a vengeance, His arms flinging wild
Guilty, you're guilty, guilty he cried.

Gethsemane

Darkness falls around Him

as he bows his head to pray

His friends keep watch that fateful hour

though they cannot stay awake.

Let this cup pass by me,

in torment Jesus cries

through anguish, bloody sweat appears

upon his furrowed brow.

Kneeling on the cold hard ground

not my will but thine be done

so the glory of the father

is revealed through me your son.

The sound of soldiers' footsteps fill the air that's cold and crisp

as Judas stands before him and betrays him with a kiss

thirty silver coins he's paid to deliver him to die

as His life hangs in the balance by those Pharisaic lies.

The Trial

The trial started early

I was there within the crowd

They brought in Jesus bound with chains

Then threw him to the ground.

They mocked him and made fun of him

I couldn't make a sound

He looked at me from where he lay

As silence fell around.

The angry mob surrounded him

Tormenting him with words

Then through the silent agony

That fateful sound was heard.

The cockerel crowed not once but twice

As Jesus had proclaimed

They said "you're with this Nazarene

I denied I knew his name.

Jesus said, "I tell you, Peter, the rooster will not crow this day,

until you deny three times that you know me."

Matthew 26 verse 34

The Upper Room

The candles all flickered,
casting shadows around
we had hidden ourselves in sorrow and fear
Trying to not make a sound.

Feeling alone in that cold upper room
frightened and lost and dismayed
It seemed an eternity there in that place
Since my Saviour and Lord went away.

Then all of a sudden, a strange, sweet perfume
Descended and covered the room
Jesus was standing there; His arms open wide
Wanting me to examine His wounds.

Then he said to Thomas,
"Put your finger here and look at my hands.
then reach out your hand and put it in my side.
Stop your doubting and believe!"

John 20 verse 27

The Lily

Standing by the water
where the lily used to float
Just dreaming of the yesterdays
Of words I used to quote.

Just staring at the water
and the ripples at its heart
Reminds me of the yesterdays
Reflections of the past.

Love

Love is as a flower in full bloom

Its softly painted petals and its strong and sweet perfume

Its beauty cannot be reckoned with, or scent compared with hue

Love is as a flower, a beautiful, wonderful flower

Love is as a flower, a flower such as you.

Water to wine

We were at the feast in Cana

Just nestled in the throng

The wedding host came up and said

The wine was all but gone.

Mary asked of Jesus, "Is there nothing you can do?"

My time has not arrived yet, " What is this to do with you"

She called the servant over, do whatever he may say

He told them "Fill these jars with water, these jars of earthen clay."

Then Jesus had them take the wine,

to the steward of the feast

the wine was served to all the guests

The important and the least

And when the wine was tasted

by each and every guest

the lesser wine had been served first

for this wine was the best.

On the third day there was a wedding in Cana of Galilee, and the mother of Jesus was there. Jesus and his disciples had also been invited to the wedding. When the wine gave out, the mother of Jesus said to him, "They have no wine." And Jesus said to her, "Woman, what concern is that to you and to me? My hour has not yet come." His mother said to the servants, "Do whatever he tells you." Now standing there were six stone water jars for the Jewish rites of purification, each holding twenty or thirty gallons. Jesus said to them, "Fill the jars with water." And they filled them up to the brim. He said to them, "Now draw some out, and take it to the chief steward." So they took it. When the steward tasted the water that had become wine and did not know where it came from (though the servants who had drawn the water knew), the steward called the bridegroom and said to him, "Everyone serves the good wine first, and then the inferior wine after the guests have become drunk. But you have kept the good wine until now." Jesus did this, the first of his signs, in Cana of Galilee, and revealed his glory; and his disciples believed in him.

John 2:1-11

The night sky

A boy stands by a window
It's ten o clock at night
Just staring at the blanket of stars
In the moons radiant light.

He stood by the window for hours
Eleven then twelve o clock passed
He looked at the clock it was half past one
Then suddenly a comet flew past.

The minutes just melted to hours
The clock chimed a quarter to three
He lay on his bed with a smile on his face
Just thinking of all he had seen.

Time

Time waits for no man
No woman or little child
It continues through the ages
Through space and mind and kind

Its silent but not still
Its careful yet has a will
A will to move a will to stand
Time waits for no man.

The Chapel

The old chapel stands there empty now
With its locked and shuttered door
cobweb covered Bible
And dusty broken floor.

The hymnals all lay tattered
with their songs of yesteryear
where once a throng of people stood
is empty now, I fear.

People talked about revival
though I fear it's come and gone
a worldwide lack of faith appears
where once it stood so strong.

The prodigal

Working for years by the sweat of my brow

weeding and tilling the land

there must be a world, something better than this

a life full of pleasures for man.

I will go to my father and tell him I'm leaving

to make it out there on my own

give me what's mine, I will say to him pleading

My inheritance and that which I'm owed.

I left for the city, I travelled the world
I had friends I had women and wine

But they soon disappeared when my money was gone

I ended up living with swine.

Then it came to me clearly, one night in the cold

My father's servants, live better than this

I will return to my home and ask his forgiveness

with a hug and a hope and a kiss.

I was still a way off, down the old dusty road

A road I had wandered and roamed

My father caught sight of me off in the distance

and ran up and welcomed me home.

The Widow's mite

We were sat on the steps of the temple

just enjoying the cool of the day

as some people gave of their offerings

and others were kneeling to pray.

The merchants and Pharisees, all dressed to the nines

dripping in silver and gold

publicly lauded their offerings

but then came a widow of old.

Just two copper coins, are all that she had

as she placed them inside of the bowl

all that she owned in the palm of her hand

oh what a sight to behold.

It's easy to give when your wealthy

But this widow, so faithful and true

gave all she had, as the Pharisees scoffed

"We are so much better than you".

But God doesn't look at the outside

He sees what we have in our heart

for the last will be first in the house of the Lord

and those who are first shall be last.

Faith as a mustard seed

When the storms of life appear

And life seems so dark and so grey

when the road ahead isn't clear

And mountains just stand in your way

When Life seems to deal you an unfair hand

And each day is filled with worrisome need

Mountains will move at your spoken command

if you have faith as a mustard seed.

*"Have faith **in** God," Jesus said to them. "Truly I **tell** you that if anyone says **to this** **mountain,** 'Be lifted up and thrown **into the sea,'** and has no doubt **in** his heart but believes that it will happen, it will be done for him. Therefore I **tell** you, whatever you ask for **in** prayer, believe that you have received it, and it will be yours....*

Mark 11 verses22 - 24

Unclean

He was there on the hillside, just teaching the crowd,

So I made my way to Him; and fell on the ground

Lord, I know you are able to heal me today

just give me the words and I'll be on my way.

unclean I would shout as I stumbled on by

my voice would be trembling and weak

but there on that hillside in front of that crowd

My skin became perfect and clean.

He looked in my eyes with a love I'd not known

I'm willing he said with a smile

all were astonished when he reached out his hand

and my skin became that of a child.

Noah

Noah was a builder he built a wooden boat

Then filled it full of animals and prayed that it would float

He led his wife and family inside, God sealed the door

The rain came down upon the land and lasted forty days or so.

Then when the flood was over, he sent a little bird

Out across the water to find itself a perch

The bird returned without a doubt, in its feet a branch

Noah took some cows and settled down and started up a ranch.

Lazarus

We were still a way from Bethany,

When Jesus got the news,

Lazarus, His friend was dead,

Was there nothing we could do?

We made the journey onward,

with sadness in the air,

four days we travelled wearily,

until we saw them standing there.

Mary and Martha, her sister,

full of sorrow and sadness inside,

Lord if you only had been here,

Our brother would never have died.

Lazarus rise and come forth Jesus cried,

in a voice that was tender yet loud,

then suddenly movement, from inside the tomb,

as he appeared in his burial shroud.

Do unto others

Do unto others, as you'd have done to you,

be honest, and gentle and kind,

for a treasure it is, to love one another,

a treasure that few rarely find.

Hold up each other, in love, faith, and prayer,

for the race, you will finally win,

Hold up each other, show that you care

regardless of colour of skin.

Do unto others in times of adversity,

offer a hand or a heart

for we all get discouraged and all feel depressed

Compassion is only the start.

Do unto others in times of great wealth

without any malice or guile

give to your brother, in times you see need

Share what you have with a smile.

Matthew 25 verse 45

Then he will answer them, saying, 'Truly, I say unto you, as you did not do it to one of the least of these, you did not do it to me.'

Printed in Great Britain
by Amazon

21629795R10020